We ♡~~Hate~~ Team Projects!

A Friendly, Useful Guide for College Student Teams

Scott Behson | Stephen Bear

Kendall Hunt
publishing company

Cover image © Shutterstock.com

www.kendallhunt.com
Send all inquiries to:
4050 Westmark Drive
Dubuque, IA 52004-1840

Published in the United States of America

Contents

A Letter to Our Students

In your careers, you will need to be able to work effectively in teams.

However, in our years of experience teaching classes that involve student teams, it has become clear to us that most student team projects are not helping you develop the team-related skills you need, and, more often than not, are turning you off from future teamwork.

This is why we all hate team projects!

You may hate team projects because, all too often, some get stuck doing all the work, and since no one is in charge, there is little you can do about this. Further, because many professors stay "hands-off" when dealing with student teams, you get little day-to-day guidance on how to navigate tricky situations and develop successful team processes.

We are tired of seeing our students struggle. That is why we have written this book.

In these pages, you will find lots of usable information about team dynamics that are specifically applied to the challenges faced by student project teams. You will read about success and disaster stories our students have faced, as well as advice on what you could learn from them. Finally, you will find lots of easy-to-use assessments, templates, and forms that you can use in your teams to set yourself up for success.

Ultimately, we want you to succeed in your team projects—and having a better team process will help you get there. A better team process will make your projects more enjoyable and will help you gain skills that you will absolutely use in your careers.

Here is how we recommend you use this book: read the content, and use all of the templates to keep yourself on track. However, if you cannot cover everything, the following 10 activities should be most helpful:

1. Hold an initial team meeting to get to know each other, as an icebreaker.
2. Fill out the roles and responsibilities template.
3. Develop and agree to team ground rules, using the template.
4. Hold a team meeting at least every 2 weeks, using the agendas and minutes templates.
5. Over the course of the project, have each team member fill out two accountability reports to share with the team.
6. Plan out your project using the project map template.
7. As a team, fill out the half-time assessment form and hold a meeting to discuss it.
8. As a team, fill out the after-action review.
9. If the professor wants peer feedback for grading, provide the templates for this.
10. After you are done, do something fun to celebrate!

We wish you good luck this semester and are confident that, if you use these concepts and templates, you are much less likely to hate your team project!

A Letter to Our Faculty Colleagues

It is likely that you assign team projects in at least some of your classes.

In some, you are trying to develop your students' teaming skills, and in others, team projects are simply a means to learning concepts or analyzing cases. Sometimes, you provide structure and guidance to student teams. Sometimes, you stay uninvolved, believing that students should learn by trial and error in managing themselves. Some of you are experts in, or teach, classes involving team dynamics, whereas others have different areas of expertise and may not have the background or inclination to help manage student teams.

Whatever your situation, you probably have come to share our view that most student teams are not as effective as they can be and that a significant number of student teams end in disaster. This turns students off and prevents them from getting the most out of their projects.

We all want our students to succeed. That is why we have written this book. Assigning this book should give you more confidence that your students will have a useful and friendly guide for the road ahead.

This guidebook provides a quick review of key concepts of team dynamics, applying them to the specific situation of student project teams. It also contains examples, assessments, and templates students can use to manage their team dynamics.

You can use this book in a few ways:
- If having students develop their knowledge and skills in teamwork is a learning objective for your course, we would suggest assigning teams most, if not all, of the readings and templates in this book.

- If, instead, you want teams to manage themselves, and your priority is that you want to be kept up to date on team progress and/or problems, we would recommend that students provide you with the templates listed above in the student "top 10 list."
- If you simply want the teams to use the principles and templates of this book on their own, please encourage them to do so, multiple times and with enthusiasm.

Whatever your approach, we strongly recommend you, a few times during the semester, allocate 15 minutes of class time for student teams to have quick check-in meetings. You can assign them a template to fill out during that time or simply allow them to meet.

This small donation of class time will help your students be more successful in their projects and will communicate to your students that you support their success. The fact that you care means a lot to your students.

Finally, you may want your students to use this book in multiple classes throughout your academic program. This book's resources can be a great way to create consistency in how team projects are assigned, managed, and scaffolded within a program. Feel free to reach out to us for advice.

Introduction: Team Development

Your professor just announced that you have a team project. Yippee! We can feel your excitement. Part of your grade in this class is now dependent on other students!

So, how do you get from being a bunch of random classmates with different goals and working styles to developing into a successful team? We are glad that you asked. This book is here to help.

Before we get into specifics, let us start with a quick overview of **Tuckman's Model of Team Development**. According to this model, most temporary teams pass through five distinct stages: forming, storming, norming, performing, and adjourning. And the sequence of stages even rhymes! (Well, mostly.)

In the **forming** stage, individuals are brought together and officially become a team. Usually, students do not think much about the forming stage, but how teams are formed can have implications for your work and success down the line. This book will give you some idea about how to manage this initial phase.

Storming refers to the sometimes bumpy first experiences the team has together. Before a team can function at its best, it needs to work through disagreements and differences in working styles and perspectives. Many teams struggle with setting up schedules to meet, agreeing on how to divide the work, and who, if anyone, will be in charge. Conflict is inevitable, and sometimes, this can be uncomfortable. However, working through conflicts is often a necessary step to realize better performance later on. We will discuss several ways to handle conflict and progress to the next stage.

In the **norming** phase, teams agree on their goals and how they will be achieved. But the true buy-in to team goals only comes after working through the conflicts of the storming stage and formalizing your common understanding. This book will provide you some decision-making tools and some ideas on how to make team norms explicit and how to enforce productive behavior later on.

Most teams only **perform** their best after progressing through the first three stages. So we encourage you not to rush with your projects and to instead spend the first few weeks focusing on forming, storming, and norming. We have seen too many teams launch right away and then have major problems pop up near the deadline. We understand the urge to be productive, but this lack of patience leads too many teams to gloss over the forming, storming, and norming stages. It is better to work through those problems first.

Of course, even if you storm and norm very well, problems do emerge. We will help you stay on track while you do the bulk of the work on your projects. In this section, we will provide you some tools for managing your projects, keeping team members accountable, stopping free riders, and running productive team meetings.

Finally, when teams **adjourn**, they take the opportunity to reflect on what they learned, what went well, what did not, and what could be done better next time. Presuming that your team has been at least somewhat successful, this is also a great time to celebrate success and acknowledge the new friendships that you have made.

This book is organized according these stages, but do not worry, this is not a boring textbook. It contains ways to think through common problems at each stage and will give you some easy-to-use templates to greatly increase the chances that your team project experience will be a good one. Maybe it will even get you to hate team projects a little less.

WE HATE ♡ TEAM PROJECTS! A Friendly, Useful Guide for College Student Teams

PART 1

LAYING THE FOUNDATION FOR SUCCESS

"If you want to go fast, go alone.
If you want to go far, go together."

— African proverb

Chapter 1

Getting to Know You: Forming

Your mission in this stage is to develop team cohesiveness. Doing so will make the work in the later stages easier, more productive, and more enjoyable.
Your specific goals for the forming stage are as follows:
1. Understand the pros and cons of how your team was put together
2. Get to know each other
3. Learn about cohesiveness, and how you can start building it
4. Assess individual and team skills, strengths, and weaknesses

1. WHAT IS YOUR ORIGIN STORY?

There are a variety of ways student project teams are formed. Often, the professor asks students to form teams on their own. Sometimes, they randomly place students. Sometimes, they form teams with an intent to create diversity in terms of demographics or subject-matter expertise. There is no one best way—each approach has advantages and drawbacks. So, what kind of team are you a part of?

I am in a self-formed team with a bunch of my friends

This is good in that you already know each other and are likely to get along well. You may also have an easier time coordinating schedules, especially if you have other classes together or are on the same sports team, for example.

While this arrangement is the one most students prefer, there are some common problems with these teams. First, the fact that you are already friends may mean that you will feel pressure to get along as opposed to speaking up when you disagree (a problem known as **groupthink**). Also, friends do not always make good teammates—we've had more than a few students confess after a team project went bust: "chose my friend to work with even though I knew he was unreliable, but then I felt awkward calling him out on it, so I let it slide." Finally, these teams sometimes rush through the early stages, thinking that forming, storming, and norming are less needed—leading to problems down the line.

The best way to deal with these potential problems is to commit to really good storming and norming. In this way, you get beyond surface agreement and have deep discussions on how you are going to run your team. We will cover both the big decisions you will have to make and some ideas on how to make team decisions in the next chapter.

I am in a team with strangers

When students form their own teams, some end up with teams with three best friends and two random classmates who happened to sit near them—this is what is known as a **team fault line**. Fault lines split teams into two or more subgroups, based on characteristics like age, gender, ethnicity, background, interests, or preexisting relationships. These types of teams have the potential to exclude the perceived outsiders, making them reluctant to assert themselves. You may also need to address scheduling issues, for example, in situations in which you have four on-campus students and one commuter student, or differences in working styles when, for example, you have three US students and two from other countries.

Mixed teams need to redouble their efforts in integrating themselves by fully committing to the forming stage and should set up decision-making processes where everyone feels safe speaking up.

I have been randomly assigned

In most of our classes, we use a technique to distribute students so that each team has a mix of majors, roughly equal gender composition, as well as relatively equal distribution of other characteristics, such as commuter/on-campus, English fluency and national origin. We usually do this to force students to pay attention to forming, storming, and norming and to avoid the problems with self-selected teams. We know other professors who randomly assign students to teams.

These randomized teams face the additional hurdle of developing cohesiveness and of coordinating schedules. We will discuss these challenges throughout the book.

I have been strategically placed

For some classes, it is important to have a mix of academic backgrounds or specialized skills. For example, a computer animation class may need to ensure teams consist of both art students and computer science majors. An entrepreneurship project should ensure teams have members with expertise in finance, marketing, and management. The downside to this approach is that teams will need to understand each other's working styles and unique points of view before the team can perform at a high level.

Every type of team has its own set of advantages and disadvantages. Knowing these up front can help you as you progress.

2. GETTING TO KNOW YOU

Once you are put together as a team, it is important to learn a bit about each other and spend a little bit of fun social time together.

We believe in this so strongly that in our classes, we set aside time during class so that new teams can socialize. If your professor does not, make sure you make this happen. Some teams go to get coffee together, others go to the student union to play ping-pong, and others bring in cards to play Uno. Here is one of our favorite stories of how a student team used a game to get to know each other and build cohesiveness:

> **Jenga Squad**—This team brought in the game Jenga and used it as an icebreaker. As each student took their turn removing a block, they had to say something about themselves. The one who made the tower fall had to disclose something more personal. In this fun way, the students got to know a lot about each other. In fact, they had so much fun that they named their team "Jenga Squad," and they always played a quick game before each of their team meetings throughout the semester. Their icebreaker laid the foundation that helped this team earn an A in their service-learning project in which they organized volunteers and collected needed supplies for an area animal shelter.

Breaking the ice

We usually also use class time to lead a few icebreaker exercises. Some of our favorites (besides Jenga) include the following:

- **Two truths and a lie**—In turns, you each disclose three things about yourselves. Two of these are true, and the other is a lie. For example, I have a teenage son who hates team projects, have been on both MSNBC and Fox News, and once lived on a houseboat (for the first author, the first two are true and the third is a lie). You can repeat this exercise several times until the "lies" become harder to identify.
- **Guess who**—Everyone writes down four cool and interesting things about themselves on slips and places them in a bowl (I have had students share things such as "I studied abroad in France," "When I was a kid I was in a TV commercial," "I have seven brothers and sisters," "I have a hairless cat."). Team members take turns picking a slip from the bowl, guessing whose fact it is and why they have made that guess.
- **One shining moment**—Team members share peak moments in their lives—when they achieved something or had their happiest moments.
- **Desert island**—Team members talk about the five objects that they would most want to have with them if they were shipwrecked on a desert island. Follow-up rounds can limit choices to categories, such as food, books, movies, or video games.

There are literally thousands of icebreakers that you can choose from. A quick Google search can help you find many very quickly.

3. STARTING TO FEEL LIKE A TEAM

Team cohesiveness is the degree to which members value their membership in a team and are willing to work together to reach team goals. Cohesive teams are more likely to work well together, help each other out, have fewer conflicts, be more motivated for team success, be more committed to the team goal, and, perhaps most importantly, have more fun.

It is easier for a team of friends or of people from similar backgrounds to feel cohesive, whereas it is harder for teams of strangers or those from different backgrounds to feel so. But your beginnings are not destiny—there are several things a team can do to build cohesiveness.

It is important to spend some time on building cohesiveness in the beginning, because this is a window of time where patterns of behavior often get set. Here are some of the things that help your team build cohesiveness:

Spending social time together, especially early on

You cannot feel like a team until you spend time together. Of course, as you will be working together, you will spend some time together in meetings or on your tasks. But work time by itself is not enough to build strong bonds. It is also important to spend social time together, getting to know each other and learn about each other in a more relaxed setting. This is part of why icebreakers are so effective.

Here is one of our favorite stories of how a student team built cohesiveness:

> **Team Treadmill**—This team consisted of two outgoing student-athletes who knew each other very well and two shy international students who were in their first semester in the USA. The two athletes did their cardio workouts in the campus fitness center in the hour before our 10 a.m. class. They invited their two new teammates to join them, and the four of them ran treadmills together before class the rest of the semester. This team aced their international business project, and we are happy to report that, 3 years after graduation, they are all still really good friends.

Spending enough work time together

One big mistake that we see many teams make is that they come together, quickly divide up the work, and then bring their work together only just before the deadline. Of course, this means that if one member does not do a good job (or does not do their work at all), the others do not know this until it is too late. But this is also a bad system because having regular work-related interactions also maintains cohesiveness.

Having regular "check-in" meetings are important not only to stay on track (as will be discussed in Chapter 4) but also to maintain personal relationships and show commitment to teamwork. For example, many of our student teams build in 5 to 10 minutes of social time (or Jenga time) into the agendas of their team meetings or make it a point to have lunch after class once a week.

Creating common ground

Spending social and work time together tends to reveal important underlying similarities, making surface differences less important. Only by spending time together, you can overcome the challenge posed by having diverse teams and members who do not know each other prior to working together.

Remember that team that ran treadmills together before class? It would have been easy for that team to feel like two separate groups and act that way. However, they created an opportunity for regular social interaction which helped them see that, despite their different backgrounds and personalities, they valued each other and could work well together—leading to high team cohesiveness.

Nothing succeeds like success

While cohesiveness can lead to team success, success also helps teams feel more cohesive. One of the best things we can do in a team project is to set early **short-term goals** and then work hard to accomplish them. By achieving a short-term success, your team will start to feel more confident in each other and be more likely to work hard for continued success. We will discuss how you can embed short-term deadlines and goals into your teams in a later chapter.

In our classes, we often make student teams work on a silly in-class assignment together to jump-start this process. For example, we give newly formed teams 25 minutes to come up with a team name, a motto, a logo, and a haiku (a non-rhyming Japanese poem consisting of five syllables in line one, seven in line two, and five in line three) about the importance of teamwork. They then have to present their work to the rest of the class. This helps teams see how they work together and experience an early win, helping to build cohesiveness. Your professor may not do something like this in class, so your team may want to develop a chance for a small win early on.

One quick warning

Too much cohesiveness can become a bad thing. Students on teams with very high cohesiveness can sometimes feel pressure to go along with the team, as opposed to speaking up when needed. After all, who wants to be the jerk who messes up your great team chemistry? This tendency to go along, called **groupthink**, can mean that very cohesive teams sometimes do not have enough debate before making decisions. All told, cohesiveness is a good thing—just be careful it does not lead to undue pressure to say you agree even when you do not.

4. ASSESSING YOUR TEAM

Aside from building cohesiveness, it is also important that you use the forming stage to determine what assets you have that can help you complete a successful assignment. You may not have been able to control your team composition, but it is important to see what skills, abilities, and working styles are contained in your group, so that you can better know and plan around your team strengths and weaknesses.

For example, your Marketing Communications class team assignment may be to develop an idea for a new product, devise a marketing plan, and give a presentation as if you were pitching your product to potential investors. To accomplish this, you would need the following: creativity, prior business classwork, marketing expertise, financial acumen, skill in business writing, organization skills, team leadership and oral presentation skills. It is unlikely that any one person is great at all of these. This is the whole point! Well-run teams allow us to be more successful than we could be working alone.

We recommend that, after you spend some time on icebreakers and cohesiveness, you use your first team meeting to break down your team assignment into its component parts, identify the skills/knowledge needed for each part, and then discuss who in the group has strength in a particular area.

Also discuss the areas in which team members may not be strong in and/or would like to improve. We have made it easy for you—use the template at the end of this chapter.

By going through this exercise, you will better understand your task and what is required, and, more importantly, will have a quick inventory of your team's collective strengths and weaknesses. This will help you divide up work, set up a work plan, and share leadership.

SUMMARY

By taking the time to take the forming stage of team development seriously, you will set yourself up for success. You will better know your teammates, feel more like a team, and better understand the challenges you face and the skills you have to address them. You have now built the foundation to allow you to confidently move forward. Moreover, your effort in this stage will make you less likely to hate your team project!

Template 1.1 Team Strengths/Weaknesses Inventory

The tasks required by the project:

The skills required to accomplish these tasks:

Individual project-related strengths and weaknesses

Name	Strengths	Weaknesses

As a team, here are our strengths and weaknesses:

Here are our areas of concern (e.g., skills needed that we do not feel strong in):

Implications of the above analysis for team roles and parts of the project certain members will take the lead on:

WE HATE ♡ TEAM PROJECTS! A Friendly, Useful Guide for College Student Teams

Chapter 2

The Big Decisions: Storming

> **Your mission in this stage is to have the hard discussions on major topics—such as team goals, leadership, structure, roles, and responsibilities—that will set your team up for success and to do so in a way that is both honest and respectful.**
>
> Your specific goals for the storming stage:
> 1. Understand the typical big decisions that need to be made before a team starts performing well, and the pros and cons of different approaches
> 2. Develop productive ways to debate, argue, and discuss important topics as a team, even when there is substantial conflict
> 3. Learn different ways to make decisions so that everyone gets on board

ENTERING THE STORM

Once your team has successfully completed the forming stage you should know a bit about your teammates and feel some connection with them. Before jumping into the work of your team project, you need to discuss important issues such as team processes, goals, leadership, roles, responsibilities, and decision-making. These discussions may be challenging. Team members may argue strongly for their points of view, cliques may form, and discussions can become intense as ego, power, and team success are in the balance. This is the storming stage.

1. MAKING THE BIG DECISIONS ON HOW THE TEAM WILL WORK TOGETHER

Here are some of the most important decisions that teams will have to make together:

Team goals

To be successful, teams must agree on how they will work together. It starts with developing a common understanding of your team's goals and those of each team member. Do you want to get an "A," or do you want to do the minimum amount of work to get a passing grade? The answer to that question can lead to radically different levels of work and commitment, and it is important not to assume that all team members have the same goals. A student taking a course in his or her major, or a student trying to maintain a high grade point average to keep a scholarship may have a strong commitment to achieving an "A," while a student who is not interested in the subject matter or who has significant outside work responsibilities may simply want to pass the course. People may have other goals—work on a new skill, make new friends, etc.

Understanding and resolving potential differences in team goals will be crucial to success and may be a strong indicator of how willing everyone is to work on the project. You should have an honest discussion about this topic during one of your first team meetings. By being up front, you can avoid big problems later.

Team leadership

There are many questions to answer about team leadership. Will the team have a formal leader—someone who all team members recognize as the leader and who has authority to lead the team—or will all team members have equal authority and responsibility for governing the team? Having a formal leader may make team management and decision-making easier, while working without a single formal leader may encourage everyone to get involved.

If there is a team leader, do you want a single leader for the whole project or do you want to rotate leadership? It often makes sense to allow whoever is doing the most work on a certain part of the project to become the "leader of the moment." For example, if one takes the lead doing preliminary research, she or he can also be the leader for the next team meeting. When another teammate steps up to be the primary author/editor, he or she can take the temporary leadership role. This arrangement obviously requires lots of communication to coordinate.

Finally, how will you choose your leader? Will there be a formal vote, or will you allow a leader to emerge as the group navigates the storming stage?

Roles and responsibilities

It seems obvious that teams need to identify roles and responsibilities for the work that needs to be accomplished, whether it be a research report, science experiment, marketing plan, or financial analysis.

Many class projects involve conducting research, performing some sort of analysis, and then documenting this work in a paper and in-class presentation. Not everyone is good at all of these things. Not everyone is particularly interested in all of these tasks. That is OK—actually, it is the reason why team work can make us more successful than working alone.

If you use the template in Chapter 1, it can help you identify interests and strengths so that you can assign roles with these in mind. Having people work in areas that are their personal strengths may enhance the quality of the project, while having people work in areas where they need to develop and grow may increase learning. You can also pair up those who are strong in an area with someone who wants to learn—creating a fun way to perform and improve.

Further, some students have time constraints due to team travel schedules, work, internships, or other classes. Not everyone can be a lead player all the time. By being organized about your work roles and responsibilities, it is more likely that everyone will do their fair share of the project and can step up when their role is most needed.

Notice we said "fair share" not "equal share." Ideally, everyone does an equal amount of work, but in practice, some have more interest, skill, and ability than others, and it is OK if, consistent with individual goals, some do a little more or less. This is true as long as the team agrees on this up front, instead of failing to live up to expectations later on.

It may be less obvious that in addition to agreeing on who will be responsible for producing the work of the team, teams must also agree on roles and responsibilities for the work process the team follows. Teams need someone to set meeting agendas, take meeting notes, publish meeting minutes, manage project timelines, and communicate with team members on an ongoing basis. Some but not all of these responsibilities may fall to the team leader or team organizer, while other roles and responsibilities will have to be defined and assigned. There is a template at the end of this chapter that can help you identify and assign roles, and get everyone on board with what they are responsible for.

2. ENSURING THE RIGHT KIND OF CONFLICT

It is important for a team to recognize the difference between **constructive and destructive conflict**. When conflict is constructive, ideas are debated instead of people being criticized, usually leading to better solutions. In fact, constructive conflict usually leads to better solutions and avoids the problems with groupthink. In destructive conflict, team members are personally challenged, and the conflict produces a competitive situation when team members want to win rather than find the best solution.

So, how can we make sure, especially during the storming stage, that our potential conflicts and debates over goals, roles, and leadership are constructive conflicts? It requires a shift in our thinking.

Contrary to popular belief, most conflicts do not arise over things like personality. In fact, conflict and disagreement are usually based on different people having **different expectations** and not fully seeing things from the others' point of view. (Yes, there are some very difficult people out there—about 5% of people are unrepentant jerks. You can usually work well with the other 95%. If you are stuck with a jerk, it will not be fun, but you can consider it good practice for the workplace!) Here is a scenario:

> During an initial team meeting, Lois (who was on a disastrous team last semester when several teammates slacked off, sticking her with all the work) wants to make sure the team meets in person every week. Clark (who is a busy student-athlete and was on a team last year where everyone worked mostly independently and the project worked out just fine) strongly disagrees. Tempers flare as Lois assumes that Clark is a slacker, and Clark thinks that Lois is a control freak. Things get nasty. Their teammates Lex, Diana, and Bruce are horrified.

It turns out Lois and Clark likely do not disagree on the overall goal of having a productive team and getting a good grade. But they have different expectations for how the team should get there. Because they do not explain their expectations or ask the other about theirs, tempers flare and conflict gets personal.

Had they explained their expectations and listened to each other, they probably could have worked out a solution that they could both be happy with—for example, by holding frequent team meetings in the beginning and loosening up as long as the project is going well, or scheduling fewer meetings but committing to checking in with a team text every day.

We find the first exercise at the end of the next chapter really helpful in getting teammates to discuss their past teaming experiences and understand each other's expectations. In it, teams discuss the qualities of the good and bad teams that they have been a part of in the past, and then discuss ways to stay on the right track.

Once you have a disagreement, you can handle it in one of several ways—these **conflict-handling strategies** vary based on how much you assert your priority versus how much you consider the other's priority. Being very **assertive** in handling conflict (all about your priority, no consideration of others') could ensure a decision goes your way but usually with a major cost to the relationships and team dynamics involved.

Almost all of the time, it is better to combine some consideration of both points of view. This likely leads to a **compromise** solution, where you meet in the middle, or finding a new creative, **collaborative** solution that makes everyone happy. If some issues, for which you do not have a strong opinion, are important to a teammate, you may just want to **accommodate** them to keep things going smoothly—but be careful you are not frustratedly staying quiet because of peer pressure (remember groupthink from the previous chapter). If you disagree, a constructive conflict conversation, while sometimes difficult, is almost always worth it.

3. MAKING DECISIONS AS A TEAM

Good teams are effective at debating project process and content, and they encourage participation from all team members. Before meeting to discuss the key issues outlined in the storming phase, it is a good idea to have one or more team members set a meeting agenda (more about running effective meetings in Chapter 4). The agenda will provide focus, ensuring that the major issues are discussed.

If your team has not selected a team leader, consider having someone fill the role of a **meeting facilitator**. This person can ensure that the agenda is followed and that everyone has a chance to share their ideas. A facilitator can also help avoid some common problems in group discussion, including one person dominating the meeting, rude behavior, leaving people out of the conversation, and **groupthink** (i.e., when the desire for team harmony results in team members not challenging ideas that are flawed or that require debate).

A good facilitator will recognize these issues and encourage full group participation when important issues are discussed. Another good technique is to stop a conversation before the team makes a decision in order to go around the team one more time, making sure everyone can say what they want to say.

Another technique that often helps in decision-making is assigning someone the role of a **devil's advocate** (DA). The DA is responsible for coming up with arguments against the ideas that the team is considering. This means everyone has to back up their opinions, making it more likely that the team will decide wisely. It also temporarily slows down decision-making, especially in teams that may have groupthink issues. Plus, the DA is not doing this to be a jerk—they are just doing their job so that there is constructive conflict without getting mad at each other.

Finally, how do you decide? After constructive debate, there are several approaches that a team can use to make decisions. Teams can agree on **delegating** certain decisions to the team leader or to the people responsible for certain parts of the project. For example, the team might appoint a project editor who has the final say over grammar and spelling, and PowerPoint slide font and graphics. A single decision maker will reach decisions faster and will be time efficient, but there is a risk of poor decision-making (no one checking if they are doing things right) and reduced creativity.

The team may choose to make decisions by taking a vote and accepting the decision of the majority. This "**majority rules**" method of decision-making is efficient and gets all team members involved. However, it does have disadvantages, as it can create a "win–lose" dynamic with those in the minority feeling that they have lost. You also should consider whether to have **secret voting** (i.e., write your choice on a piece of paper and have someone collect them) or visible voting, such as raising hands or saying "yes" or "no." If groupthink is an issue, secret votes may be useful; otherwise, the more open, in my opinion, the better.

Finally, you may choose to require the unanimous agreement of all team members. **Unanimous decisions** ensure alignment but leads to a slower process—in fact, it may not always be possible. Often, teams agree to strive for unanimity but also agree that if a decision cannot be reached in a specified period of time, they will come to a **consensus** that everyone can agree to or will use a majority vote.

Most teams use a combination of approaches, for example, delegating smaller decisions to individuals taking the lead in those areas, agreeing to accept majority decisions for most items, and reserving unanimous decisions for only the most critical issues that the team must decide.

NAVIGATING THE STORM

It is important that you give yourself adequate time to navigate the storm. Some issues may be resolved quickly, while others may take more time. Teams should be alert to the following problems:

1. The team skips the storming phase

Some teams jump right into the work of the team project without making time to discuss team goals and team processes. Because work starts right away this seems efficient, but it actually can result in lengthy project delays if major disagreements come after project work is underway. When team members are not aligned on team goals and when good team processes are not created, the team may have to make major corrections to its work later in the project or may find that the disagreements that emerge are very hard to resolve.

2. The team sails through its first meetings without a storm

Some teams quickly agree on team goals and processes without any real debate or conflict. Again things appear to be working efficiently, but there is a real risk that difficult problems and conflicts will emerge later in the process or that work may have to be redone or substantially modified.

Alternately, one or more team members exhibit **passive-aggressive behavior**. These team members hide their disagreement and anger, but, in reality, they resent the decisions being made. The result is potentially hostility, cynicism, and a lack of commitment and engagement.

3. The team capsizes during the storm

It is possible that a team may not be able to discuss and debate issues constructively, and a high degree of frustration or anger is the result of the early team meetings. In this situation the team never successfully completes the storming stage. This can result in a divided team with very poor work processes or even a team that dissolves before the project begins. If this happens, go see your professor for advice.

SUMMARY

The storming stage is challenging because conflict is inevitable and may make some team members uncomfortable. It is not always easy, but by setting up a good team process, trying to understand each other's expectations, looking for compromise or collaborative solutions, and agreeing on how your team decisions will be made, you will be better at keeping conflicts constructive. This will likely make your team perform better while being a better experience for everyone.

Template 2.1 Big Decisions

Team:

Team Member Names:

Based on extensive team discussion, here is how we have decided to operate as a team:

Team Goals
We are on a mission to achieve the following goals as a team:
1.
2.
3.

Team Metrics
We are going to measure our effectiveness as a team through these measures:
1.
2.
3.

Team Leadership
This is how we decided our team leadership roles and structure:

Team Accountability
These are the ways we agree to hold ourselves and each other accountable for getting work done:

Team Cohesiveness

We are aware of what enhances team cohesiveness and positive interpersonal relationships within the team. We have adopted the following strategies and activities to ensure we spend social time together and develop warm and functional work relationships:

WE HATE ♡ TEAM PROJECTS! A Friendly, Useful Guide for College Student Teams

Template 2.2 Roles/Responsibilities

Team Name_____

Team Leader_____
(provides overall direction and leadership for the team; may run team meetings or may delegate this to a meeting facilitator)

Meeting Facilitator_____
(sets and sends meeting agendas, facilitates the meeting, monitors and provides feedback on team member behaviors during the meeting, sends note on meeting agreements and follow-up items)

Devil's Advocate_____
(challenges the group consensus with arguments counter to those the group is considering in order to ensure a full range of options is considered)

Project Manager_____
(develops the overall timeline for the project, sequences tasks, monitors progress and alerts the team to potential problems that could cause delays or missed deadlines)

Editor_____
(revises written documents and presentations to ensure appropriate organization of the material, ensures proper grammar, spelling, and punctuation, and ensures consistency and logic of arguments and conclusions)

Other_____
(other roles and responsibilities that the team identifies as important for team success)

Other_____
(other roles and responsibilities that the team identifies as important for team success)

Chapter 3

Getting on the Same Page: Norming

> **Your mission in this stage is to come together with a common understanding of how your team will operate, including making a commitment to the team's success.**
>
> Your specific goals for the norming stage:
> 1. Share good and bad teaming experiences
> 2. Develop a set of team ground rules to which all team members agree
> 3. Making your commitment to team success explicit

MAKING THE INFORMAL FORMAL

If your team has been productive in the storming stage, not only do you understand the big decisions your team must make, but your team has also found productive ways to debate, discuss, and argue, and to make team decisions. You worked through the potential problems and now can come to agreements more easily.

To make the transition from a collection of individuals to a team committed to collective success, you need to develop a set of **team norms**, a set of agreed-upon informal rules for how a team ought to work together.

Actually, it is even better to make your informal norms formal by having specific conversations around how you want to work together, putting them down in writing, and using them to stay on track. Here is how you can do it.

1. LEARNING FROM BOTH GOOD AND BAD EXPERIENCES WITH TEAMS

The title of the book recognizes that a significant percentage of your past teaming experiences have not been so great. But the reality is that team experiences in life, school, and work are a mixed bag—some great, some good, some OK, and some lousy.

Our past experiences, especially the bad ones, can help us going forward. First, you should recognize that you bring expectations to your new team based on past good and bad experiences—which may differ from teammates' experiences and expectations. Talking through these gets everyone on the same page. Even more importantly, discussing your good and bad experiences provides a road map for how your new team should or should not operate.

In our classes, we set aside time for teams to discuss their good and bad experiences. Your professor may not, so we encourage your team to call a meeting and use the first template at the end of this chapter to do so.

Start by discussing the successful teams you have been part of. Sharing good experiences reinforces the potential benefits of working as a team and can set a positive mood.

For example, we have had students share positive experiences including the following:
- I had a personal problem last semester, but the team was willing to be flexible with me about my part of the project. We made it work.
- Whenever we had a disagreement, we decided to put it to a vote, and all went along with the decision.
- Sometimes, after meetings, we would all stay late just to talk as friends.
- Everyone did their parts 3 days before the deadline so that we never had to rush at the end.
- By using Google Docs, we could all see and comment on each other's work even if we did not meet as frequently.
- We had a team leader who was so great at keeping everything organized.
- We took our time to decide who would do each part of the project so that everyone did an equal amount and could use their strengths.

As you discuss good teaming experiences, you will discover some common themes—good communication, organization, everyone doing their part. You will also uncover strategies that you can adopt for your own team. For example, "That's a great idea. Let's use the 3-day-early rule for our project," or "We should use Google Docs, too." It will also alert you to important team dynamics. For example, "How can we make sure everyone does their part?"

Next, talk about bad experiences. It can be cathartic and surprisingly quite helpful. Often, these discussions center on problems with **free riding** and the reality that some team members do all the work while others shirk their responsibilities. Additionally, problems with poor communication and ineffective **project management** are often identified (We will give you some guidance in the next few chapters, as well.). Some specific examples from our students are as follows:

- This one person always needed to have her own way and was a real problem when she could not.
- We set up a group text, but two people never checked in.
- One person handed in her part late, and it was terrible, so I had to rush to fix everything. So aggravating!
- We had six students in our team, and it was really hard to find a time when we could all meet.

By openly discussing past problems and disappointments your team can identify issues that may need to be addressed and then make a commitment to work together to avoid these problems. The next step is to think about past experiences and create a set of team ground rules to keep your team on track.

2. GROUND RULES RULE!

Ground rules are a road map of how the team will work together and help set expectations for individual members. Commitment to team ground rules enables a team to hold each other accountable for the quality and timeliness of their work. Equally important, ground rules enable teams to hold each other accountable for how they will work with each other. They encourage team members to listen to each other, to respect different points of view, and to engage in constructive debate.

Start by identifying the core values that will guide how your team works. Values that teams typically consider include excellence, earning an "A," respect for each other, learning, personal growth, having fun, and trusting each other. Teams should discuss why each value is important and how it will help the group achieve its goals. Then the team should agree to the list. This list should be long enough to cover what the team believes and short enough to be remembered when the team works together.

Once the team has agreed on its core values, it can translate these values into concrete team ground rules. For example, valuing excellence may lead to ground rules like committing to meet deadlines, providing constructive feedback, and asking for/providing help to ensure the best possible project. The specific ground rules can also be based on your discussions of past good and bad teaming experiences.

Most sets of team ground rules include the following:
- Expectations on meeting attendance and team member communication
- The process by which members are held accountable
- How decisions will be made and conflicts resolved
- The importance of meeting deadlines
- How team members will treat each other

We recommend using the template at the end of the chapter to record your ground rules. As an example, here is a set from one of our recent student teams:

These are the values and behaviors that each of us should exhibit as a member of this team:
- Listening to each other with an open mind and without interruption
- Respect of each other's time and opinions
- A responsibility culture, not a blame culture
- Integrity, honesty, and accountability
- Have fun and use this project as a learning experience

Based on these values, these are our team ground rules:
- Be on time to meetings and come prepared
- Listen while others speak and wait till they are done talking before you begin to talk
- Be respectful in every way
- Make decisions as a group
- Work must be completed and on time
- If there is disagreement, it should come up during meetings and decided as a group
- If someone does something wrong, it should be brought up respectfully and in private
- Answer the team group chat in a timely manner
- When setting due dates, have a due date a few days before the real due date to allow room for team members' lives
- NO FREE RIDERS!

3. MAKING THE GROUND RULES REAL

Team ground rules will not matter unless every member of the team commits to them. After your team establishes and writes down its ground rules, we recommend you hold a meeting where every team member officially signs the ground rules document and pledges to follow them.

We know this sounds silly, but psychology shows that even the simple act of publicly agreeing makes it more likely you will follow through on that agreement. We have also seen this work in practice.

One faculty committee I (the first author) joined had terrible team dynamics—people talked over each other, showed disrespect, and a few members dominated team discussions. Because of this, the committee wasted a lot of time, and no one felt motivated. After joining, I suggested that we develop a set of team ground rules. Some thought this was a stupid idea, but I persisted. We developed a set of ground rules (mostly around communication, conflict, and respect), and at the next meeting I handed out the sheets to everyone, and we signed them.

I then assigned myself the informal role of "**process cop**." During the next few meetings, when someone would violate team ground rules, I would jump in and say something like, "We all, including you, agreed to these ground rules. Let us get back to them, please." After a few meetings, I hardly needed to jump in, and very soon, the team was far more respectful. The lesson—ground rules work, if you all agree to them and then keep each other accountable.

SUMMARY

Norming is the payoff for the hard work you have done in the forming and norming stages. Team discussions about past good and bad experiences can help you develop your team ground rules. These rules are a key to success—be sure to formalize them, agree to them at a team meeting, and hold each other accountable. By doing so, the odds of good team process go way up, making it far more likely you will both perform well and enjoy your team experience.

CHAPTER 3 TEMPLATES

Template 3.1 Good/Bad Team Experiences

Team name: _____

Based on our team discussion, here is a list of the qualities and actions taken by the successful teams we have been part of in the past:

Based on our team discussion, here is a list of the qualities and actions taken by the unsuccessful teams we have been part of in the past:

Based on the qualities and actions listed above, here are aspects of the successful teams we want to re-create in our team project and how we might do so:

Based on the qualities and actions listed above, here are aspects of the unsuccessful teams we want to avoid in our team project and how we might do so:

Template 3.2 Ground Rules

Team name:

Team members:

Team Values
These are the values and behaviors that each of us should exhibit as a member of this team:

Based on these values, these are our **team ground rules**

Signatures:

By signing below, I agree to the team ground rules

_____   _____

_____   _____

_____   _____

PART 2

EXECUTING SUCCESSFULLY

"Do or do not. There is no try."

—Master Yoda

Chapter 4

Dividing Work and Keeping on Task: Performing, Part 1

Your mission in this stage is develop a project plan and timeline, using simple and easy-to-use tools to keep your team on track for successful (and less stressful) completion of your project.
Your specific goals for the performing stage:
1. Understand the different types of team interdependence
2. Harness the power of deadlines and short-term goals
3. Use project management tools to stay on track
4. Run efficient, effective meetings

1. HOW WILL YOU WORK TOGETHER?

There are three different styles you can use in doing your team work:

Pooled interdependence

We have seen some teams divide up work early in the process and then simply combine their work right before the due date. This may sound like a good way to move faster and avoid all the messiness of coordinating schedules, working through conflicts, and sitting through meetings. But this is usually not a great approach. You fail to develop cohesiveness and miss opportunities to learn from each other (and have fun!). You also get no updates on how your teammates are performing their task—are they slacking off, have they gone in a weird direction, do they know what they are doing, or did they do their work at all?

Serial interdependence

Assembly lines work like this. One person does their part of the work and then passes it off to the next. Then they do their part and pass it along (and so on). Many of your projects may be set up in multiple stages that build on each other, so you will likely use this from time to time. However, as with pooled interdependence, you can miss out on collaboration and accountability if you simply work as a chain of individuals.

Reciprocal interdependence

In this style, all team members work together, sharing ideas and making decisions, every step of the way. They even do most of their work collaboratively, including research and writing. It is great to work together, but sometimes, this style is too much of a good thing. Teams need to be cohesive, meet often, share ideas, help each other, and hold each other accountable—and this requires some reciprocal interdependence. We recommend lots of this style for you and your teams. But an over-reliance on doing everything together slows teams down and can be frustrating.

So which style should you choose?

All of the above!

Most successful teams use all three styles as appropriate. Consider a political science project in which a team needs to conduct a literature review, develop hypotheses, construct an exit survey for a local election, collect data, analyze it, report results, and provide conclusions (and, of course, write the whole thing up and give an in-class presentation).

> This team will likely begin with **reciprocal** interdependence as they proceed through the forming, storming, and norming stages. However, once they start performing, they may divide the project into individual tasks and work separately. First, the two best research-ers may take on the literature review portion and then hand off their work to the team (**serial**), who will then make a team decision on hypotheses and research design (**recip-rocal**), the best survey designer may work alone to develop a great instrument (**pooled**) and the team as a whole will refine it together (**reciprocal**). Each team member can go to a different polling station and collect data (**pooled**) and enter their data into a shared Google spreadsheet (**pooled**). The best number-cruncher can do the statistical analyses

and pass them on to the team to develop conclusions together (**serial** to **reciprocal**). The team can divide up some of the writing and presentation planning (**pooled**) but bring it all together with a week to spare to integrate all of these parts into a coherent product (**reciprocal**). One or two members may take the lead in editing the document at the end (**serial**), and the entire team participates in the presentation (**reciprocal**).

As you develop your timeline and project management map (covered later in this chapter), you will see which parts of the project lend themselves to each type of interdependence. You should also ensure that, even if you are using pooled and serial for much of the work, you have enough team meetings to allow for the coordination, accountability, and cohesiveness benefits of reciprocal interdependence.

2. THE POWER OF DEADLINES AND SHORT-TERM GOALS

Nothing focuses your attention like a **deadline**. It is human nature. So if a professor gave you a team assignment due in 10 weeks, we bet a graph of your time spent per week on the project would look something like Figure 1:

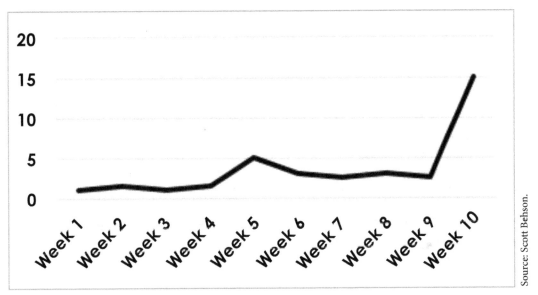

Figure 1 Hours per week

That is 4 weeks of not very much; a small burst at the half-way point when you realize you are behind, and work in fits and starts; and then a superlong week at the end—including a possible all-nighter.

We all do this, but we also know it is not the best way to work.

What if, instead of only focusing on the final deadline, we broke the project up into parts and set a deadline for each one? Then, we might have a chart that looks more like Figure 2.

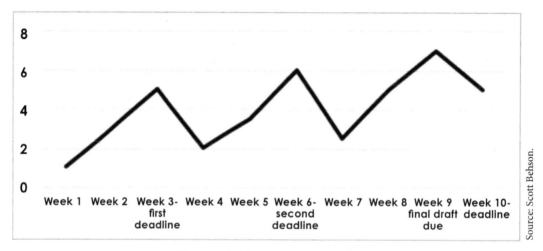

Figure 2 Hours per week

In this scenario, we have set three other deadlines before the final project is due. The power of deadlines means that you will wind up with several bursts of work and motivation before the end. As a result, the last week will not even be that stressful. You will be better able to schedule your time around other class projects, exams, and extracurriculars. And there is one more main benefit—each deadline is a chance to assess your team performance.

If your team has met the first deadline, it is time to celebrate, recognize those who did a good job, and move on to the next deadline with more confidence and cohesiveness.

If your team has not met the first deadline, there is time to recover, and figure out what went wrong and what you could do better. Maybe someone misunderstood the assignment; maybe someone started free riding. Now you can start dealing with these emerging problems now before it is too late.

One of the best things you can do for your team project is to break the big project up into smaller parts and build short-term goals around completing these parts. And we do this using just a little bit of project management.

3. PROJECT MANAGEMENT

The best way to start managing the timeline of your project is to do some **backward planning**. You start by asking, "to complete our project on time at the deadline, what needs to be finished 1 week before?" And then keep working backward until you figure out your **critical path**, the sequence of essential tasks that need to be done on time to meet the project goal.

A team project for an undergraduate course in marketing might be to come up with a line extension of an existing product, conduct market research for it, develop a marketing plan, write a 10 to 12-page paper, and make a 20-minute in-class presentation.

If the presentation and paper due date are at the end of 10 weeks, we might be able to break things down like this:
- Week 10—Deadline for paper and presentation

But, as your presentation is likely based on the completed paper, you probably need to complete the paper by Week 9 so that you have a week to put the presentation together.
- Week 9—Paper completed

In order for the paper to be completed, we need the marketing plan completed, and enough time to finish our market research. Of course, the marketing plan is dependent on the research being finished.
- Week 7—Marketing plan completed
- Week 5—Market research completed

Before we can start the market research, we need to develop our new line extension. Of course, this also includes reading, brainstorming, and coming to a team decision.
- Week 3—Line extension product selected

And, of course, in order to begin working together well, we need to go through forming, storming, and norming.
- Week 1—Begin team process work

This is a simplified example. Each section of the project will then require multiple subtasks, and you need to divide the work, roles, and responsibilities in order to get these done. You also need to set up a meeting schedule and determine your short-term goals. As an added bonus, by breaking down the project, you will see that you have to get moving quickly to reach your goals. This will help you avoid procrastination.

Once you determine what needs to be done, we recommend listing the subtasks under each main item, putting in a start/end date, and determining who on your team is responsible for each subtask.

Share out this project management plan so that everyone knows their parts, when things have to be done, and can hold themselves and each other accountable. The easy-to-use project map template at the end of this chapter can help you do this. You can also use the Gantt chart function in Excel to create a map of your own.

4. RUNNING EFFECTIVE MEETINGS

We hate meetings. We bet you do, too. Actually, we do not hate all meetings, just the unnecessary, poorly planned, poorly run meetings that do not accomplish anything. Some days, it seems like all meetings are that way. But they do not have to be. Here are a few simple tips for running good meetings—meetings that run on time, are well-organized, and get things done.

First, remember what meetings are really for. They are <u>not</u> for getting work done. Everyone should be getting their work done, alone or in subgroups, in between meetings. The meetings are a checkpoint to review work, solve problems, make decisions, and set a plan of action. They can also be important for building cohesiveness. Overall, a good meeting is one that respects everyone's time.

Planning for a meeting

For meetings to be effective, there are a few things that need to be done beforehand. First, you need to send everyone an **agenda**, preferably several days ahead of time. Your agenda lists the items that you will discuss and decide upon during the meeting. It will also list what team members need to accomplish and share out before the meeting. Without an agenda, people cannot be prepared and, as a result, meetings turn out to be long, frustratingly inefficient, and a waste of time.

Using our example of the team with the marketing project, a good agenda for their Week 5 meeting could be as follows:

AGENDA
Meeting Date: March 18, 6 p.m. to 7 p.m. in the Student Union Coffee Shop
- 7:00—Share good news/social discussion
- 7:10—Review and discuss the draft of the market research report prepared by Tommy and Alicia. Come to final decisions for T/A to finish up
- 7:40—Determine next steps for putting together marketing plan. Who will be in charge? Who will assist?
- 7:55—Debrief and final thoughts

To be done before the meeting:
- Tommy/Alicia—share your draft in the team Google Docs 5 days before the meeting
- All—read, review, and have your ideas and suggestions ready; continue on your own tasks

---

WE H̶A̶T̶E̶ ♡ TEAM PROJECTS! A Friendly, Useful Guide for College Student Teams

With this agenda, it is much more likely everyone will come prepared, having done their work—this is especially true because the agenda mandated the report to be posted several days before the meeting. This means that this team can have a great discussion and efficiently make decisions. Also, notice how they built in time in the beginning for socializing or cohesiveness-building, and some time at the end to make sure everyone can express themselves. We provide an easy-to-use format for agendas and meeting minutes at the end of this chapter.

During the meeting

In Chapter 2, we discussed lots of different roles team members fill. One of the most important is **meeting facilitator**. This can be your team leader but does not have to be. In fact, most teams we have had in our classes rotate the role so that everyone gets a chance.

In addition to developing the agenda, the facilitator should take responsibility to keeping the meeting focused and on time. If your social discussion starts going too long, it will reduce the amount of time you can spend on the main task (or, worse, make the meeting go long). The facilitator should speak up when discussions are going longer than the allotted time and alert the team. The team can decide to move on or make the active decision to spend more time on the current topic.

The facilitator should also monitor how team members are treating each other. If someone is talking over other people or drifting off, the facilitator can keep everyone in line. The best way to do so is keep a copy of the team ground rules handy and point out to a team member if they are breaking a rule. The facilitator can also point out when conflict turns destructive and try to get people to debate more constructively.

Finally, the facilitator should take **meeting minutes**—short notes on what was discussed and decided up at the meeting, and should prepare a list of action items to be done before the next meeting. For our marketing team, the minutes may look something like this.

MINUTES
Meeting Date: March 18, 6 p.m. to 7 p.m. in the Student Union Coffee Shop

Alicia, Tommy, Carlos, and Lea present, Jee-Yon was absent but had let us know ahead of time and had sent everyone his notes on the market research.
- It was Lea's sister's birthday yesterday. Tommy's team won their season opener. Carlos got a haircut (looking hot! LOL)
- We discussed the market research conducted by Tommy and Alicia. We all agreed that they did a great job, and made the following small suggestions:
  o See if we can divide the data from the focus group between men and women—there may be relevant comparisons here
  o Be sure to quantify the feedback in terms of totals and percentages

---

- o We need a thorough copy-edit for grammar and writing style—Carlos volunteered to help
- We determined Lea and Jee-Yon would take the lead on developing the marketing plan and that they would work on the draft using the Google Docs so that we can all comment on it in real time over the next 2 weeks.
- Because Alicia has a little extra time this week, she will begin putting together some of the PowerPoint slides, making a first stab at the format and style we will use.
- Tommy pointed out that his soccer team is traveling the next two weekends, so he may be a little harder to reach. He will be sure to dive into the project more later in the semester.

Action Items
- Next meeting April 2, same time and place
- Lea and Jee-Yon will have a good draft of the marketing plan by March 27 for us to discuss during next meeting and will share on Google Docs
- Carlos will copy-edit the market research report
- Alicia will share her PowerPoint draft and ideas
- Spring formal this Friday!

Tommy did a great job! Thanks to these minutes, everyone (including Jee-Yon) know what happened at the meeting, the decisions that were made, and who is responsible for what going forward. This is a great way to ensure the team works well and meets deadlines. It also makes it much harder for a slacker to hide in the group. In fact, if a team member is a consistent problem, these minutes could be useful for sharing with your professor.

SUMMARY

Now that you have broken down your project into parts, set short-term deadlines, scheduled meetings, and decided what level of interdependence you need for various parts of your project, you are well on your way to making sure your project will stay on schedule, that is, if everyone does their part. Ensuring that this happens is the topic of the next chapter.

Template 4.1 Project Map

Part 1. First, determine which major project tasks have to be completed by the following dates:

Final project due date: _____
What needs to be finished by then?

1 week before the due date: _____
What needs to be done by then?

2 weeks before the due date: _____
What needs to be done by then?

3 weeks before the due date: _____
What needs to be done by then?

4 weeks before the due date: _____
What needs to be done by then?

5 weeks before the due date: _____
What needs to be done by then?

6 weeks before the due date: _____
What needs to be done by then?

7 weeks before the due date: _____
What needs to be done by then?

8 weeks before the due date: _____
What needs to be done by then?

9 weeks before the due date: _____
What needs to be done by then?

10 weeks before the due date: _____
What needs to be done by then?

Part 2. Next, working your way from the bottom of the chart in Part 1 to the top, list each part of the project, the date you should begin working on it, the date it should be finished by, who will be responsible for that task, and other important information:

Task	Begin date	Finish date	Who is responsible?	Notes

Task	Begin date	Finish date	Who is responsible?	Notes

WE HATE ♡ TEAM PROJECTS! A Friendly, Useful Guide for College Student Teams

Template 4.2 Meeting Agenda

Meeting date/time/place:

Items to be discussed:

Work that needs to be completed and shared with the full team 5 days before meeting:

Copy of minutes from prior meeting (distributed at least 5 days before meeting):

Template 4.3 Meeting Minutes

Meeting date/time/place:

Members in attendance:

Items discussed:

Decisions made:

Action items for the next meeting, including who is responsible for each:

Next meeting date/time/place:

Chapter 5

Holding Each Other Accountable: Performing, Part 2

Your mission in this stage is to ensure that everyone contributes to project success and are held accountable for their effort and progress toward both task completion and positive team dynamics.

Your specific goals for the performing stage:

1. Use individual and team progress reporting to ensure everyone can track each other's efforts
2. Give regular positive and affirming feedback
3. Understand the predictors and symptoms of free riding and social loafing
4. Develop successful strategies for dealing with a situation in which a team member persists in free riding

1. MARKING PROGRESS

The project management and meeting tools in the last chapter should help you get and stay on track. It is also really important that each team member holds themselves accountable to the rest of the team by periodically recording what they have done for the project over the past few weeks. Doing so creates a record of what has been accomplished, by whom, and can help you update your project management plan over time.

There are easy-to-use templates at the end of this chapter for individual and team progress reporting. We recommend having all team members fill out an individual progress report every 2 to 3 weeks, or when there are major deadlines. A progress report will look something like this:

Team: Alias Investigations Member: Trish W.
Progress Report for October 10 to 24

What I said I would do during the past 2 weeks:
- Develop agenda and take minutes for meeting on October 16
- Work with Malcolm and Jessica to complete first draft of Part 1
- Meet with professor during office hours to clarify her expectations for Part 2

What I accomplished during the past 2 weeks:
- Developed agenda/minutes for October 16 meeting
- First draft almost completed
- Totally forgot to meet with professor! Sorry!

What I commit to do over the next 2 weeks:
- Finish Part 1 draft
- Meet professor!
- Go to library and find five references for Part 2

What I need from my teammates over the next 2 weeks to accomplish this
- Remind me to go to office hours
- Have someone join me at the library
- Someone to run next meeting

Either the team leader, or the team as a whole, should also develop a team progress report. Similar to the individual report, this should list what the team said they would do to that point, what it accomplished, what still needs to be done, and what the team needs from each other to make this happen. This will be a very helpful document to keep your team accountable and on-time toward its goals. It can also be a useful reporting mechanism if your professor wants an interim report.

Halftime!

In most sports, teams compete, take a break at halftime, and then get back at it. Halftime allows teams to take stock of what went well, what went wrong, and how the team should operate in the second half. We recommend you use halftime as an opportunity to assess your team, as well as each other, so that you can move forward with purpose down the stretch.

The half-time version of a team progress report is designed to monitor and report on team process, rather than on deadlines and goal attainment (these are the focus of the individual and team progress reports described above). As such, the template at the end of the chapter includes sections on what has been going well, and what needs improvement. It also includes sections for teammates to provide feedback to each other—emphasizing positive feedback.

2. ACCENTUATE THE POSITIVE

A lot of the content in this book is about eliminating problems—minimizing the reasons we hate team projects. This will be especially true in the next section of this chapter. However, as long as we are reporting progress to each other, we should also take the opportunity to recognize the good work that most of your teammates are providing, and to highlight those who are also making your team a better, more positive team experience. The half-time report is useful here.

On the second page of that template, we include space for you to list the qualities you respect about each of your teammates and the unique talents they bring to your team. Acknowledging and then discussing the positive qualities about your teammates should help everyone feel recognized and can lead to better cohesiveness and effort.

We also recommend building **recognition** into team meetings. First, teams should acknowledge when a member meets a deadline or short-term goal. We should also recognize when a team member adds to the positive team dynamics—for example, going out of their way to include the commuter student or making your meeting more fun by introducing a new icebreaker.

Some of the teams in our classes have built in fun ways to recognize teammates. Some examples are as follows:
- One team would vote on the "teammate of the week" at the end of each team meeting. They bought a silly hat for the winner to wear.
- One team collected $10 each at the beginning of the project and used it to buy a Starbucks gift card. When each team member finished their part of the project, he or she could buy a coffee drink of their choice. The remaining money was used for a team celebration after the project was handed in.
- One team came up with a point system in which the team leader was empowered to give members points for meeting a short-term goal, and points for each time they went out of their way to improve team dynamics. The team kept count, but kept everything lighthearted, like a game.
- One team printed a bunch of "thank-you" cards, and whenever one team member stepped up, the others gave them a card.

However you do it, it will be worth your time to recognize good performance in both project completion and team dynamics. Sometimes, all it takes is a little recognition to help keep up the motivation of your enthusiastic performers.

And with that, we unfortunately turn our attention to those who do not do their fair share …

3. NO MORE FREE RIDES!

Maybe the biggest reason we all hate team projects is the we have been burned by **free riders** who do less than their fair share (and sometimes nothing!) on a project, sticking us with all of the work. Even worse, these free riders almost always get away with it! They get the same (or sometimes only slightly lowered) grades as those who work hard. Most of the time, your professors want you to work things out on your own, so they do not do much to help you out.

Free riders are basically playing a game of chicken against students who care more about their project's success and the final grade than they do. Ultimately, free riders know that other teammates will likely cave in and end up angrily doing their work for them instead of submitting a bad final product.

So, how can you prevent free riding? How can you stop it when others free ride? How do you hold free riders accountable when you are just peer classmates with no authority to fire, demote, or otherwise punish free riding?

It is not easy, and there is no 100% solution. We wish there were; we hate free riders as much as you do! But there are some things you can do to make free riding less likely, detect it early on, and maybe (just maybe) get that slacker back on track. In the next chapter, we will also talk about peer reviews that, even if they do not prevent free riding, can make it clear to your professor who in your team did not do their share—so they hopefully get what they deserve.

Preventing free riding

Malicious free riding happens when a team member actively chooses to do less in a team setting because they believe that (a) they will not be found out and/or (b) they will get away with it even if they are.

Therefore, the first way to address potential free riding is to set up conditions where everyone's efforts are visible to everyone else. Happily, we already discussed how cohesiveness, team ground rules, progress reports, and team meetings can support this goal. Conversely, free riding is more likely to happen when:

- A team does not develop enough **cohesiveness**. Cohesive teams work for a common goal. In teams without cohesion, everyone is out for themselves.
- A team works mostly in **pooled interdependence**. When team members work in isolation, the rest of the team will not know if someone is slacking until it is too late.
- A team does not meet frequently. If someone misses **meetings** or does not contribute during them, that could be your first sign that something is up. Also, team meetings are a great time to discuss **individual progress** and follow up on action plans—this can let you know if someone is falling behind. Meetings can also help maintain cohesiveness.
- A team does not establish **short-term goals** or deadlines. If someone misses their first few short-term goals or deadlines, you still have time to address the problem before the project is due. If you wait too long, it is too late.

In short, a lot of what we have covered in earlier chapters will also help you prevent free riding or spot it early on.

Before we talk about dealing with free riding when it happens, we should also note that there are other, less malicious, circumstances in which a team member may not contribute their fair share. These other ways of slacking are sometimes called **social loafing**. Besides free riding, social loafing takes a few other forms:

When a team member does not feel, even if they tried, that they can help the team

For example, let us say there is a team in a computer science class with three seniors who are CS majors and a new transfer student taking his first CS class. The newbie may understandably feel he does not have much expertise to offer, so he hangs back, stays quiet, and does little. After all, he thinks that his effort will not move the needle on the project. (We have also seen this happen with non-native English speakers, exchange students, and non-majors in teams with more expert students.)

In cases like this, it is up to the other team members to address this concern with empathy and see if there are other ways the newbie can contribute. After all, this person is not a malicious free rider—they just do not see how their efforts can make a difference. Maybe the newbie is a good writer, presenter, meeting facilitator, or project manager and can help the team with these skills. Maybe he can be paired with one of the experienced members so that he can learn and become more confident.

When a team member does not feel like a true part of the team.

In Chapter 1, we discussed some issues in team formation that can lead to **fault lines**, or for individuals to feel less valued than other teammates. For example, an introvert in a team of extraverts can feel as if they never get a word in during meetings and that the team rushes through decisions without getting their opinion. A commuter student working with on-campus students may not be able to attend some meetings and may miss out on cohesiveness-building social interactions.

In both of these cases, teams that take their time during forming, storming, and norming should be able to anticipate potential problems, and take action to compensate. For example, the first team can ensure that, before decisions are made, all team members have a chance to give their final opinion. They should also redouble efforts to actively facilitate meetings so that everyone has their voices heard. The second team could create asynchronous ways to collaborate (group texts, Google Docs), and also have the on-campus students go out of their way to accommodate the commuter's schedule.

4. DESPERATE TIMES CALL FOR DESPERATE MEASURES

All of the advice in the previous section should be super-helpful. However, it will not eliminate free riding in all cases. The most malicious free riders only respond to negative consequences. As class-mate peers, you do not have control over punishments. It is possible, but unlikely, your professor has given you the authority to severely reduce a teammate's grade or to "fire" a deadbeat teammate. If so, you have a stronger hand. If not, there is only so much you can do. So, what can we do with an unrepentant free rider?

Early intervention

If your professor spells out a procedure in your syllabus about how to handle a free rider, follow those instructions. In addition, we recommend that you also do a few more things.

Thanks to the fact that you are providing periodic progress reports, and you have been holding meetings and checking performance against short-term goals, you likely have good documentation of your free rider's pattern of poor performance.

You should use early evidence of free riding to have a firm, honest but polite team meeting to address your concerns before things get out of hand. At this point in the project, you should lead this conversation with empathy. After all, perhaps this teammate is struggling with a personal issue, is not aware that they are as behind as they are, or has different expectations on team performance (see Chapter 2).

Remember that this initial conversation should be one of **constructive conflict**. Stick to the facts—missed deadlines and their effects on other team members' work—rather than focus on personal accusations like, "You're a slacker!" Make it clear that continued missed deadlines will result in informing the professor, leading to a reduced grade and/or the initiation of a "firing" procedure. But also make it clear that the rest of the team is there to help support the free rider in coming back to the pack. Something like this:

So, Julia, we've noticed that you missed the last two team meetings and didn't get your part done by the agreed-upon deadline. This affects the rest of us because we don't know if we can expect you'll meet the next deadline or are 'plugged in' to what's going on with our team.

We need everyone pulling together. Is there something going on that we should know about that's getting in your way? Is there anything we can do to help you get caught up? *(and really listen!)*

We need to be able to count on you. We're all filling out progress reports before our next meeting—I really hope yours will show you are catching up. If you are, then everything's cool and we're back on track. If not, we're going to have to talk to Dr. B about what to do next.

Document, document, document

Be sure to document this meeting in your minutes. Also, hang on to all your progress reporting, meeting minutes, project management plans, etc. (Your professor may need these in the event that they hear a different story from the free rider later on.)

Talk to your professor!

After your meeting, your team leader should talk to the professor so that this issue is on his radar. *(We cannot emphasize this enough!!!!!!)* If you let professors know about issues early on, they are much more likely to be willing and able to help. Last minute cries for help may be too late. Complaining only after the fact means your professor cannot do anything even if she wanted to. Involve your professor early on, even it if is just a quick heads-up that a problem could be developing!

If all else fails

If you can fire a free-riding teammate, follow your professor's advice on beginning that process.

If you cannot and things continue to go badly, you may want to start cutting your losses. Your expectation should now be that the free rider will no longer contribute. Hold a meeting to divide the free rider's work and make sure the rest of the team can get the project done. It is totally unfair, but with enough lead time, it probably will not be too onerous for a team of four or five to make up for one free rider. If the free rider comes back to the team, treat this like an unexpected bonus. You can give them a few small, less critical tasks to complete before trusting them with more extensive work.

Finally, in many team projects the professor asks for peer evaluations so that they better understand the relative contributions of team members. Some use these to adjust individual grades within the team. For example, in most of our classes, we use peer feedback to adjust individual grades up to +10 for the top performers and up to −20 for the free riders. That means, a team grade of B+ could mean a 97 for a star and 67 for a free rider. Most professors do not adjust grades as extensively. We will discuss peer evaluations and provide you two templates in the next chapter.

SUMMARY

Most of the previous chapters focused on setting plans for success. This chapter focuses on making sure this plan is executed well. By making sure everyone regularly reports their progress, recognizes good performance, and addresses free riding (the #1 reason we hate team projects!), you are more likely to end up with a successful outcome—and a much more fun team experience.

Template 5.1 Individual Accountability Report

Name, Team: _____

What I said I would do over the past 2 weeks:

What I accomplished: (What caused a discrepancy, if any?)

What I commit to do over the next 2 weeks:

What I need from the team to ensure I meet my goals:

Template 5.2 Team Accountability Report

Team:

What we said we would do by (date) _____:

What we accomplished: (What caused a discrepancy, if any?)

What we commit to do by (Date) _____:

What we need to ensure we meet our goals:

WE HATE ♡ TEAM PROJECTS! A Friendly, Useful Guide for College Student Teams

Template 5.3 Half-Time Team Assessment Instrument

Name, Team: _____

Fill out this form individually, and then share your thoughts in a 30-minute team discussion to collaboratively determine your plans going forward

How happy are you with the progress your team is making toward researching, writing, and presenting an excellent team project?

Source: Scott Behson.

Please explain:

How happy are you with your team's dynamics (how well do people get along, make decisions together, hold good meetings, communicate in between meetings, listen and respect each other, show up, live up to your ground rules, etc.)?

Source: Scott Behson.

Please explain:

Please list three things that are going well with your team:

1

2

3

Please list three things that the team needs to improve upon going forward:

1

2

3

Here is one thing I really respect about each of my teammates, and one thing each of them can do, based on their unique talents, to help make us a truly great team:

1. _____ :

2. _____ :

3. _____ :

4. _____ :

5. _____ :

Please write the name of each teammate in the appropriate category. Some categories may contain many names; others may contain none:

1. Deserves special recognition for their outstanding contribution so far	
2. Doing more than their fair share	
3. Doing their fair share	
4. Doing less than their fair share	
5. Are being hindrance to the team	

For the people you list in 1, 2, and 3 above, what could you or your team do to recognize their positive performance?

For the people listed in 4 and 5 above, how can you or the team act to fix the situation and get these members back to be involved and motivated?

Considering the above questions and our team discussion of them, here is our plan going forward for work, and for team dynamics:

Chapter 6

Closing Your Project: Adjourning

> **Your mission in this stage is to look back on your team process and performance, learn from your experience, and celebrate your success.**
>
> Your specific goals for the adjourning stage:
> 1. Understand the importance of team debriefing, and know how to conduct this assessment
> 2. Conduct honest and respectful peer evaluations
> 3. Celebrate project success

WOO-HOO! WE ARE DONE

You handed in your project and made your presentations! Congrats on getting it all done.

Well, actually, there is just a little bit more you should do to get the most out of the team experience. You should take some time to reflect on what you learned, what went well, what did not, and what could be done better next time. You can provide each other (and often the professor) feedback on how well each member performed. Finally, presuming your team was generally successful, this is also a great time to celebrate success and acknowledge the new friendships you made.

1. THE TEAM DEBRIEF

Did your team project go as well as you hoped it would, or was it a disappointment? If successful, you will want to understand why so you can be successful again. If you did not achieve your goals, you will want to learn from the experience so you can do better the next time. This is why it is so important to conduct a **team debrief** at the end of every project.

You may be interested to learn that many organizations from major corporations to the US Army conduct team debriefs (often called **after-action reviews**) in which they discuss what was supposed to happen, what actually happened, and why things happened. The purpose is to improve future performance by learning from the team's experience.

Make sure to conduct your debriefing as soon as possible after the project is completed, so that the project and your experiences are fresh in your mind and you can accurately reflect on the team's work. To conduct the project review, first have each team member complete the after-action review template found at the end of this chapter. Then gather all the team members to discuss their observations in a team meeting. Ask your best facilitator to lead the meeting in order to consider key questions including what was supposed to happen, what actually happened and why. Consider both the team's final project and the team's dynamics or working relationships. Identify those things the team did well and those things the team could have done better from both a project and a working relationship standpoint. Finally and most importantly, capture the lessons learned from the experience and indicate what you can do differently on future projects.

Your meeting should be open and honest, but should be conducted with an orientation toward learning rather than one of blame. Even if there are specific teammates who detracted from team accomplishment, there is little to be gained by directly confronting them at this point (see the next section). Instead, focus on what happened, how it affected the team, and how this can be improved next time.

For example,

> We had a problem with a team member who didn't show up to our last few meetings. This caused confusion over whether parts of the project were done, causing stress and a rushed final project. What's done is done, no matter how frustrating. But let's talk about what we can do in future teams to prevent this from happening to us again.

Rather than, "Brandon, you jerk, you really messed us up!"

One last thing—hold on to your debrief documents. You can use them when developing your good experiences/bad experiences conversation and team ground rules next semester.

2. GIVING AND RECEIVING FEEDBACK

Providing and receiving honest and respectful peer feedback is an important learning experience. Ideally, you have used the half-time team assessment instrument to provide some initial feedback to your teammates so they had an opportunity to improve their performance during your project. Now is the time to provide some final feedback to help your teammates improve in future teams. The templates at the end of this chapter are good tools to accomplish this.

Be candid and respectful, recognizing that to learn and grow we all need honest and helpful feedback. Also, be open to feedback on your own performance. Others' perceptions may not line up with your own self-perception. Take peer feedback as a learning opportunity, instead of lashing out or being defensive.

The first of the two peer assessment forms at the end of this chapter is good for both internal team use and for professors to collect. This form is straightforward and lends itself to having frank but friendly team discussions. Even if your professor does not ask for peer feedback for grading purposes, please at least use this first form as a team learning opportunity.

Looking at the first sheet and using the example above, Brandon should receive "well below expectation" ratings for meeting attendance and timeliness of work. This feedback, given respectfully, will have impact. You do not need to yell about it in a debrief meeting.

On the plus side, other teammates probably exceeded some expectations or even demonstrated "star level" performance. This is a great opportunity to recognize them here. Please use the full scale! Too often, we have seen teams that we know had lagging members but where everyone received 3's and 4's. This is not helpful feedback for your professor, and is not good for student development.

The second peer assessment form is designed for use by professors in adjusting individual members' grades within teams. We recommend you fill out these forms individually and give them directly to your professor, as opposed to sharing these for internal discussions. This way, you can feel freer to give an honest assessment, allowing instructors to adjust grades accordingly. You will notice this second form also contains questions that force you to distinguish between individual member performance. We provide these to help you help your professor understand your relative contributions and make grading decisions.

Before we asked these types of questions, many teams, even those we knew were having big problems, would rate all team members at the same "meets expectations" level. We get it, giving negative feedback is uncomfortable. But, when teams do this, we professors have no choice but to give everyone the same grade regardless of who did more work and who took a free ride. Remember, this form goes directly to your professor, so you can be fully honest.

In our classes, we will often adjust individual grades up to +10 for those consistently recognized as star performers and up to −20 for those who detracted from the team. Most professors also adjust grades, but not often as significantly—they will usually state the grading policy in the syllabus. If you are overly lenient, or are hesitant to use all parts of the given scales, you will not give your professor the opportunity to adjust grades to recognize individual effort and performance in your team.

Remember—Use the developmental feedback forms for constructive criticism and improvement. Use the evaluative forms so your professor knows who did their fair share. Do not let free riders get away with it! Make sure star performers are recognized! Be fair to everyone!

3. LET US CELEBRATE!

If your project was a success and team dynamics were good, this is a great time to recognize everyone's hard work and celebrate your success. Even if your project was only semi-successful, there are probably things to celebrate—new friendships, lessons learned, the end of the semester. It's a small world and you may have the opportunity to work with your teammates again in another class or after graduation in the business world, so end the project on a positive note by taking a moment to recognize each other's hard work and your team's accomplishments. After all, school, work and life shouldn't be only about results—be sure to take some time to have some fun every now and then.

Many of our student teams have ended their semesters with small celebrations. Some examples are as follows:
- A night out at a local pub
- Dinner together
- Creating a fun awards ceremony—deciding on awards like "best teammate" and "team cheerleader"
- Spending the remaining money on the team Starbucks card for a round of lattes
- One last Jenga game

Finally, you may have relied on others for help in your project. Your professors or other faculty may have been good resources for you. Maybe a librarian helped you find what you needed. Some projects have you interact with outside businesses or charities. Perhaps you needed to interview people or run focus groups. Maybe other classmates gave you some encouragement or feedback, or your roommate was willing to let you practice your presentation in front of her. Part of celebrating should also involve thanking those who have helped you. You can probably think of creative ways to show your gratitude. At the very least, a phone call, email, or thank-you card is always appreciated.

SUMMARY

The learning does not end when the project does. Spend some time reviewing your performance in a team debrief and providing helpful feedback for your teammates. Peer feedback is important for ongoing development and as a way to help your professor grade individual contributions within a team. Finally, take some time to celebrate success and thank each other for your hard work. You deserve it!

A FRIENDLY GOOD-BYE

And with this, we have come to the end of the book. We sincerely hope that you have found this content useful and that it helped you have a better team experience. Maybe you did not hate your team project this time!

We hope that you will keep this book handy for your team projects next semester, the one next to that, and the semester after that. Lots of the information in this book can also help you in your careers and in other parts of your life.

Thank you so much for your time and effort! And we would appreciate any feedback that you have for us.

Template 6.1 After-Action Review

Name, Team: _____

Fill out this form individually and then share your thoughts in a 30-minute team debrief

How happy are you with the quality of your final product?

Source: Scott Behson.

Please explain:

How happy were you with your team's dynamics?

Source: Scott Behson.

Please explain:

Please list three things that your team did well from a project-work standpoint:

1

2

3

Please list two things that your team could have done better from a project-work standpoint:

1

2

Please list three things that your team did well from a team-dynamics standpoint:

1

2

3

Please list two things your team could have done better from a team-dynamics standpoint:

1

2

If we could do it all over again, here are the two things I would do differently:

1

2

A Friendly, Useful Guide for College Student Teams

Please list four lessons that you will take with you and apply in your future team projects:

1

2

3

4

Overall, these are the things that I am most grateful for from this team project experience:

1

2

3

Template 6.2 Peer Assessment Form 1

Name, Team: _____

Please rate yourself and your classmates on the following criteria:
- 1-   Well below expectations
- 2-   Below expectations
- 3-   Met expectations
- 4-   Above expectations
- 5-   "Star" level performance

Classmates →

	You				
1- Attendance at in-class meetings					
2- Attendance at out-of-class meetings					
3- Active participation in making important decisions for the team project					
4- Leadership throughout the team project					
5- Contribution to positive team dynamics					
6- Quality of work contributed to process documentation					
7- Quantity of work contributed to the project					
8- Quality of work contributed to the project					
9- Timeliness of work contributed to project					
10- Overall Contribution					

Comments:

Template 6.3 Peer Assessment Form 2

Please distribute a total of 10 points times the number of teammates (40 points among 4 team members, or 50 among 5, and so on), according to their overall contribution. Ten points for an individual would indicate average contribution, higher numbers must be offset by lowered totals for others.

Names					
Points					

Comments:

Please write the name of each teammate in the appropriate category. Some categories may contain many names; others may contain none:

1. Deserves special recognition for their outstanding contribution	
2. Did more than their fair share	
3. Did their fair share	
4. Did less than their fair share	
5. Were a hindrance to the team	

Comments:

Based on their performance on this project, rate whether you would choose your current teammates for a future important project. How would you choose?

1-   Definitely would not choose
2-   Probably would not choose
3-   Would choose
4-   Would very enthusiastically choose

Names→					

If I had to choose just one person for special recognition for their contribution on this project, it would be _____

About the Authors

Scott J. Behson is a professor of management and Silberman Global Faculty Fellow at Fairleigh Dickinson University, where he teaches a variety of organizational behavior and human resource management classes. In addition to his academic publications in the area of work and family, Scott also writes for business and popular press, including *Harvard Business Review, Time, Fast Company,* and *The Wall Street Journal,* and, his first book, *The Working Dad's Survival Guide* (Motivational Press, 2015). He has spoken at the White House, the United Nations, and many international conferences, and has appeared on *NPR, MSNBC, CBS, Bloomberg Radio,* and *Fox News.* He also provides consulting and corporate speaking services on work–family policy. Scott earned a PhD from the University at Albany, State University of New York and a BS from Cornell University. He lives in Nyack, NY with his wife, stage actress Amy Griffin, and son, Nick. Website: http://Scottbehson.com. Email: scottbehson@gmail.com

Stephen E. Bear is an associate professor of management at Fairleigh Dickinson University, where he teaches Organizational Behavior, Human Resources, Organizational Ethics, and Career Strategies. Prior to joining the faculty at Fairleigh Dickinson, Steve worked extensively in industry both in the USA and internationally. His experience includes serving as a marketing executive, a general manager, and a senior strategist—culminating in his role as the senior vice-president for human resources at Bristol-Myers Squibb. Steve earned a DPS from Pace University, an MBA from the Harvard Business School, and a BA from Duke University. He lives in Larchmont, NY with his wife Janet.

Acknowledgments

Stephen:

Most of all, I want to thank my students for inspiring me to be a better teacher and a better person. I also want to thank my family for their love and support and for encouraging me to go back to school to start a second career. I have many fine colleagues at the Silberman College of Business at Fairleigh Dickinson University whom I want to thank for their support, insight, and guidance. Finally, it has been a privilege to work with Scott to help bring to life his vision for this guidebook on teams.

Scott:

This book is dedicated, first and foremost, to my students at the Silberman College of Business at Fairleigh Dickinson University. You have taught me so much, and I am proud to have helped you navigate college, careers, and many team projects! You have made my career so fulfilling. As a small gesture of Steve's and my gratitude, a portion of the royalties from this book goes directly to the SCB scholarship fund.

Of course, this book would not have succeeded without the generous help and support of so many. My wife, Amy, and son, Nick, are constant sources of joy, clutter, adventure, surprise, and love. My parents, Joe and Grace, gave me so much, including the love of reading and writing. My colleagues at FDU have provided me a vibrant, encouraging workplace and a team of professors that I am proud to call friends. Special thanks to Drs. Rosman, Wischnevsky, Jones, Fairfield, and Hansbrough—and most of all, my coauthor Dr. Stephen Bear.

Thanks also to Melissa Lavenz, Elizabeth Palmer, and the team at Kendall Hunt, and to Dr. Josh Misner for making the introduction.

Sources for Further Reference

Many of the concepts presented in *We Hate Team Projects!* come from the accumulated scholarship of group and team dynamics in the fields of psychology and management. Most of our analysis, advice and templates stem from years of study and classroom practice—refining and combining these ideas into our own unique presentation. While we do not make many explicit references to theories and models, we would like to highlight the works of several important scholars and sources to which we owe a debt of gratitude, and that you may be interested in for future reference.

- Bauer, T., & Ergodan, B. (2009). *Organizational behavior*. Boston, MA: Flatworld Press.
  - Any good recent organizational behavior textbook, including the one we use in our classes, will have a solid chapter or two on team dynamics and managing teams
- Carr, S. D., Herman, E. D., Keldsen, S. Z., Miller, J. G., & Wakefield, P. A. (2005). *The team learning assistant workbook*. New York, NY: McGraw-Hill.
  - A workbook for student teams that accompanies an online tool. Contains lots of reflection and assessment tools.
- Cavanagh, K. (2014). *Who works where (and who cares?): A manager's guide to the new world of work*. Park Ridge, IL: Life Meets Work.
  - A practical guide for business teams, especially those who telecommute or coordinate from a distance.
- de Janasz, S., Dowd, K. O., & Schneider, B. (2014). *Interpersonal skills in organizations* (5th ed.). New York, NY: McGraw-Hill.

- A useful text for developing student interpersonal skills for future careers and management roles.

- Dyer, W. G., Dyer, W. G., & Dyer, J. H. (2013). *Team building: Proven strategies for improving team performance* (5th ed.). San Francisco, CA: Wiley/Jossey-Bass Publishers.
  - A consultant's view on helping managers get the best out of their teams.
- Fisher, R., Ury, W., & Patton B. (1991). Getting to Yes: Negotiating agreement without giving in. London: Penguin.
  - The classic text on win-win negotiating and conflict management.
- Gersick, C. (1988). Time and transition in work teams: Toward a new model of group development. *The Academy of Management Journal, 31*(1), 9–41.
  - The classic study of the importance of deadlines, half-way points and transitions for team dynamics.
- Hackman, J. R. (Ed.). (1989). *Groups that work (and those that don't): Creating conditions for effective teamwork.* San Francisco, CA: Jossey-Bass.
  - A classic study that embedded scholars in dozens of different work teams, discovering many common patterns.
- Kogon, K., Blakemore, S., & Wood, J. (2015). *Project management for the unofficial project manager.* Dallas, TX: Benbella Books/Franklin Covey.
  - A practical project management guide for non-experts—especially useful for team leaders.
- Levi, D. (2014). *Group dynamics for teams* (4th ed.). Thousand Oaks, CA: Sage.
  - A comprehensive source for team dynamics models and theories.
- Tuckman, B. W. (1965). Developmental sequence in small groups. *Psychological Bulletin, 63*(6), 384–399.
  - In which the classic forming, storming, norming, performing model is presented.

And, of course, if you'd like to use this book as a reference, you can cite:

- Behson, S.J. & Bear, S.E. (2019). *We Hate Team Projects: A Friendly, Useful Guide for College Student Teams.* Kendall Hunt: DuBuque, IA.

Printed in the USA
CPSIA information can be obtained
at www.ICGtesting.com
JSHW052234100823
46248JS00001B/1